The Twelve Traditions for All of Us

The Twelve Traditions for All of Us

Joe Klaas

Hazelden

First published March, 1986.

ISBN: 0-89486-357-6

Printed in the United States of America.

Editor's Note:

Hazelden Educational Materials offers a variety of information on chemical dependency and related areas. Our publications do not necessarily represent Hazelden or its programs, nor do they officially speak for any Twelve Step organization.

INTRODUCTION

I was gently introduced to my first Anonymous meeting in 1957. Someone greeted me at the door and asked, "How old are you?"

"Thirty-six," I replied.

"Got a job?"

"Yes."

"A car?"

"Yes."

"Wife and family?"

"Yes."

"Well," shrugged the old-timer, "you're not old enough nor destitute enough to qualify like the rest of us; however, you're lucky — we have a new rule. From now on the only requirement for membership is a desire to stop." He smiled. "So you're welcome to join."

He was saying that even though I hadn't lost my family, job, and car, I was as eligible for membership as anyone else. But it wasn't a new rule that had saved me. It was a Tradition.

Currently, I belong to several anonymous Fellowships. My compulsions are numerous enough to make me eligible for nearly every recovery program except Alateen. However, as to which groups I actually belong to, I remain anonymous. Participants in these programs go by their first names. It's not a rule. It's a Tradition.

There are no rules in the anonymous programs which have helped upwards of three million people recover from incurable diseases. How more than 300 anonymous Fellowships operate without rules is no less a miracle than the recoveries achieved by their members.

From the cradle throughout most of life, we are taught to hustle. "There's no such thing as a free lunch," is an American free enterprise cliche. We are also taught that those who hustle the most get others to hustle for them. "When you take someone to lunch, sell something."

We are also taught to become managers. The most respected people in the community are managers. If we learn how to manage fifty thousand people, we can conceivably become president of a giant corporation. *That,* we are trained to believe, is success. It is even more successful to become head of state, managing millions of people.

There are distinct sets of rules for those who manage and those who are managed. Both kinds of rules are made by the managers. They formulate liberal rules to regulate their own behavior and to achieve the greatest profits possible without going to jail. They impose rigid rules that force the multitudes they manage to work as hard as allowable under law for the lowest pay possible.

An organization run without rules would be chaotic for both managers and those they manage. Without restrictions deemed necessary to prevent failure, no one within such an establishment could be trusted to kindle the welfare, growth, and success of the enterprises.

The world is made up of millions of large and small power structures working to achieve human goals. Power is issued from the top, downward. Presidents, church officials, and boards of directors issue orders and make important decisions. Directives are pressed relentlessly downward through less and less privileged levels of management. Citizens, troops, and employees follow rules and meet responsibilities in order to achieve goals. Each level is held accountable to the one immediately above it. All are responsible to a boss or committee that has either been elected or appointed to a position of power.

From birth to adulthood, we are urged to work hard to reach the top. That system has endured since the first whimper of history, in the form of family, small business, corporation, dictatorship, and democracy. The concept of absolute power pressing downward with increasing force and diminishing benefits has carried humankind through feast, famine, accomplishment, and destruction.

The power structures that take credit for positive periods of our battered history will not accept responsibility for historical disasters, e.g., starvation, war, and oppression that have brought civilization to the brink of nuclear suicide.

In struggling for supremacy, power structures have involved the name of God. Belt-buckles of those who operated extermination camps were inscribed *Gott mit uns* "God is with us." They were hanged for their crimes by those who upheld the slogan "In God we trust." Humanity's struggle to carry out what leaders have called "God's plan" has been the bloodiest slaughters of all. The Holy Inquisition, in which millions were tortured and burned alive, lasted 496 years.

Power hierarchies may not be responsible for all miseries of history; however, the endless struggle to achieve and hold positions of power has done little to relieve the unhappiness they have caused.

There is, however, an alternative to this chain of command madness. In the twentieth century, a truly innovative structure has emerged from the least likely source imaginable. A way has developed for millions of men, women, and children, of all races, religions, political persuasions, and nationalities to work together in solving problems and accomplishing incredible objectives. This new method of achieving goals does not rely on human bosses or rules, yet, has had successes so spectacular they are hard to believe.

Today, more than 300 close-knit Fellowships are functioning beautifully. They do not compete within their own memberships or with any other organizations. Money of all denominations and nationalities is being collected, distributed, and spent to good purpose. Vast quantities of books, pamphlets, and magazines are being published and circulated. Educational programs are being offered at most hospitals, schools, and jails around the world. This is all being done without struggle for profit or power.

Every year, more and more groups of people with special problems are adopting this efficient method of human management. This method for achieving success is laid out very simply in the Twelve Traditions. The Twelve Traditions began to evolve in Akron, Ohio, in 1935, when two physically, morally, spiritually, and financially destitute drunks got together to try to stop drinking.

Bill W., one of the two Akron founders of Alcoholics Anonymous, set the Twelve Traditions down on paper. They were digested into simple form and adopted by the A.A. General Service Conference. The Twelve Traditions have been adapted by more than 300 divergent Fellowships such as Smokers Anonymous, Gamblers Anonymous, Overeaters Anonymous, Loneliness Anonymous, Al-Anon, Alateen, Adult Children of Alcoholics, Cocaine Anonymous, Mistresses Anonymous, Credit Card Anonymous, and Sex and Love Anonymous. The Twelve Traditions are also available to any other group or organization that wishes to find happiness.

The Twelve Traditions of A.A., adapted for use by any organization that wishes to apply them, are as follows:

1. Our common welfare should come first; personal recovery depends upon unity.
2. For our group purpose there is but one ultimate authority — a loving God as He may express Himself in our group conscience. Our leaders are but trusted servants; they do not govern.
3. The only requirement for membership is a desire to stop our self-destructive behavior.
4. Each group should be autonomous except in matters affecting other groups or our Fellowship as a whole.
5. Each group has but one primary purpose — to carry its message to the individual who still suffers.
6. A group ought never endorse, finance, or lend the Fellowship's name to any related facility or outside enterprise, lest problems of money, property, and prestige divert us from our primary purpose.

7. Every group ought to be fully self-supporting, declining outside contributions.
8. Our Fellowship should remain forever nonprofessional, but our service centers may employ special workers.
9. Our Fellowship, as such, ought never be organized; but we may create service boards or committees directly responsible to those they serve.
10. Our Fellowship has no opinion on outside issues; hence the name of our Fellowship ought never be drawn into public controversy.
11. Our public relations policy is based on attraction rather than promotion; we need always maintain personal anonymity at the level of press, radio, and films.
12. Anonymity is the spiritual foundation of all our Traditions, ever reminding us to place principles before personalities.*

Most groups seeking recovery from problems other than alcoholism adapt the Twelve Traditions to meet their specific needs. They simply substitute their own words such as *compulsive overeater* for *alcoholic, drugs* for *alcohol*, or *Al-Anon* for *A.A.*

The Twelve Traditions, like the Twelve Steps, are easy to understand. Believing they will work and deciding to follow them are difficult. Obeying orders from our parents, teachers, and employers may not bring us happiness; in fact, the familiarity with this old system may discourage us from trying something totally new and different.

We must pay strict attention to what the Twelve Traditions say, so as not to modify them to suit our own biases. In a quarter of a century in various Fellowships I have heard the Twelve Traditions repeatedly misquoted by individuals or

*Permission to adapt and publish the Twelve Traditions granted by A.A. World Services, Inc., New York, 1976.

groups trying to impose misguided morality on individuals or general membership. I have been guilty of this myself, and by admitting my mistakes I have learned the truth and been able to grow with the help of my Higher Power.

Many of us arrive in our respective groups with an inclination toward bigotry. We soon learn that prejudicial attitudes toward others along lines of race, religion, nationality, education, or economic standing are unacceptable in an anonymous program. The next sanctuary of discrimination is the enforcement of rules. But there are no rules in an anonymous Fellowship. What frustration! But wait . . . there are the Traditions. The hallmark of bigotry is to find ways of preventing others from doing what they want to do.

I have either invoked or heard others invoke the Twelve Traditions as laws to prevent dually-addicted persons from mentioning their "other problem." Groups have recited the Twelve Traditions to keep homosexuals from openly referring to their "relationship difficulties." The Traditions have been used to prohibit helpful literature other than "conference approved" material from being read or sold. Organizations have cited the Twelve Traditions in order to halt fund-raisers and censor announcements being made about social functions for which members must pay an admission fee. Groups on more than one continent have misused the Traditions by prohibiting members from joining hands during the Lord's Prayer or preventing a group from praying together at all. The Traditions have been used to deny Fellowship conferences and conventions from charging registration fees. Members who use first and last names at the group level, or officers whose names are printed in organization literature, have been condemned for "violating the Traditions." One time I traveled two thousand miles to attend a meeting of one of my Fellowships and was refused admission because I was a stranger and it was a "closed meeting." There is obviously room for clearer understanding of the Traditions.

I have interpreted the Twelve Traditions in just about every way they can be misinterpreted. I have learned what they do mean only by finding out the hard way what they don't mean. I seem to be one of those hardheads who only learn by making mistakes. But isn't that often how we learn the truth?

The purpose of a handbook for those who wish to follow the Twelve Traditions can only be to eliminate the pain and turmoil of making the same mistakes others have made. By examining what the Twelve Traditions do not say, perhaps we can learn together what they do say.

Any group can follow the Twelve Traditions. All it needs is a desire to live free of struggle for prestige, profit, and power. A group must be willing to place its welfare in the care of a Greater Power and its operation in the conscience of its members.

If you are ready to learn about the Traditions, turn the page and take a long look at Tradition One.

TRADITION ONE

Our common welfare should come first; personal recovery depends upon unity.

Twelve Step recovery programs conduct tens of thousands of group meetings all around the world. More than a hundred languages are spoken at the meetings. Every major religion is represented in their memberships. Those who attend come from every economic and social level of society. Members have varying amounts of formal education. Groups operate in kingdoms, democracies, and dictatorships; through war and peace, and through times of freedom and oppression. All members meet as equals because they share the same goal: they want to stop self-destructive behavior.

The largest of these Fellowships, Alcoholics Anonymous, began with two members in 1935. Through half a century, A.A. has expanded from two to two million members and shows no signs of stopping. In fact, its growth rate is accelerating as never before.

Doctors have only recently learned that to "cure" their alcoholic patients, they must prescribe A.A. Even more recently the medical community has realized that a very successful treatment for obesity is Overeaters Anonymous; and for drugs, it's Narcotics Anonymous or Cocaine Anonymous. Increasing numbers of judges are sentencing victims of addictive diseases to Twelve Step programs rather than jail.

Should A.A. continue to grow as it has over the past 50 years, members would number between one and two billion by the centennial anniversary in the year 2035. Those figures probably seem as impossible to us as it would have seemed to those first two drunks in 1935 that A.A. would number between one and two million by 1985.

On a trip deep into mainland China, during my 25th year of practicing the Twelve Steps, I suddenly realized I was in the midst of more than a billion people who had not yet heard of the Twelve Steps or the Twelve Traditions. Today, anyone traveling in China may contact Alcoholics Anonymous, Overeaters Anonymous, or Al-Anon by getting in touch with the United States Embassy in Beijing.

The biggest miracle is not that these Fellowships have expanded at such an awesome rate but that they have done so without loss of unity.

"The welfare of the whole comes first," is a time-honored principle. What is new, is that in Twelve Step programs it does come first. It comes before ambition, power, prestige, and autonomy. The unique goals of an individual or group cannot take priority over the common goal of all the groups. Each group, therefore, assumes responsibility for the continued operation of groups everywhere. Individual members, in turn, assume responsibility for the success of their group.

A group that draws itself into some small and private corner to function independently of the others is actually withdrawing from the Fellowship and the Fellowship's common objectives. An individual who seeks recovery through a Twelve Step program is most unfortunate in becoming a member of an autonomous group which regards itself as new, different, and superior to the Fellowship as a whole. The unfortunate newcomer entering such an unconventional unit will have been attracted under false pretenses.

Groups who are convinced that they have now learned to manage their own recovery are compelled to manage the lives of others. Beware of those who admit they have lost the ability to manage their lives yet proceed to dictate how you should manage yours.

Within some groups, members control each other's abstinence or sobriety by discipline. Instead of practicing the message of the Steps by turning all authority over to a Higher Power, members use surveillance to keep each other in line. Such groups can grow very large and financially independent because keeping a strict eye on one another may seem like "an easier way" than giving all power to God.

These groups may actually compete with other groups rather than contribute to their common welfare. They may try to out-recruit other groups and thus add to their combined safety in numbers. Or they may delude themselves into thinking that as the biggest and best group in the area, they are contributing to the common welfare of the Fellowship by assuming an air of leadership over all other groups. They may campaign to take control of the intergroup, central office, and the general service board. They may even try to take command of the whole program, which in effect is an attempt to replace God.

How can we keep a hundred thousand groups of a worldwide Fellowship from splintering off on a myriad of tangents? The founders of Alcoholics Anonymous devised a way for all members and groups to have a voice yet stay unified. Bill W. and Dr. Bob S. perceived that their power should be passed along not to those at the top but to those at the bottom. They may have been the only leaders in history to realize not only that they could be replaced, but also that they did not need to be replaced.

Anonymous Fellowships preserve their unity by electing a representative from each group to serve as an area committee. That representative carries the conscience of the group to the committee. Area committees elect delegates to consolidate the conscience of Fellowship groups everywhere. Employees hired by the conference of delegates coordinate national and international activities, provide information and literature to all

Fellowship members, educate the business and professional community about the Twelve Step program, and inform the public about Fellowships available to those who need them.

Thousands upon thousands who have placed their lives in the care of God "as [they] understood Him," exert their will through group representatives and area delegates. Unity prevails as God's will works through members.

The worldwide membership *is* the fellowship. The Twelve Steps *are* the program. There is not an *I*, *me*, or *my* mentioned in any Step or Tradition. The Steps and Traditions cannot be done alone by an individual. We can only do them together. Individual recovery depends upon worldwide unity.

If you agree that your own recovery depends upon working for our entire Fellowship's well-being, you are in good shape to turn the page and start examining Tradition Two.

TRADITION TWO

For our group purpose there is but one ultimate authority — a loving God as He may express Himself in our group conscience. Our leaders are but trusted servants; they do not govern.

Tradition Two consists of two parts. The first part describes God as our ultimate authority expressed through our group conscience. The second part describes our leaders as those who serve rather than govern us.

My recommendation on how to observe the first part of Tradition Two lies within the Third Step. On our path to recovery, we make a decision to turn our will and our lives over to the care of a Higher Power. The Third Step teaches us that when we put ourselves in God's care His will is expressed through us. We can practice Tradition Two by realizing that if we put God in charge He will be expressed through our group conscience.

In attempting to understand the second part of Tradition Two we may ask who will lead us if no one governs? Let us go back and have a good look at the structure of our Fellowship. After all, it was designed to keep our program spiritual.

For starters, we have individual group members allowing God to manage their lives through Twelve Steps of recovery. Members elect a secretary to serve their group. As mentioned earlier, they also elect someone to represent the group at a higher level. The representatives gather to ensure the welfare of area groups. These representatives hire employees to serve in a central office. Those employees see to the immediate needs of the area groups and send those seeking help to meetings. The representatives also elect a delegate, someone they believe to be living voluntarily in God's care, to serve the area groups at a national or international level. The delegates meet at an annual conference for the purpose of bringing the consciences of all the Fellowship's groups to bear on problems and projects affecting the welfare and recovery of members and future members everywhere. The conference hires knowledgeable employees from within and outside the Fellowship to operate a national or world service office. This office indirectly serves individual group members through delegates and area representatives.

As you can see, all direction seems to flow upward from member to group, from group representative to delegate, from delegate to conference, and from conference to a national or world service office staffed by paid employees. These employees then do what the resulting group conscience of all the Fellowship's members wish done about publishing literature, handling inquiries from individuals or groups, informing the public, educating the professional community, providing help to those who wish to start new groups, and making sure the Fellowship's hand is extended anywhere in the world when someone asks for help.

Does the power really flow upward from individual group members to a world service office? Yes, God's will is expressed through those who have turned their will and their lives over to one Greater Power.

Must elected leaders and paid employees go back to the groups to get a vote on everything they do? Of course not. Through this structure, members pass authority along to the people they elect or hire. Those people are chosen because they follow Twelve Steps and Twelve Traditions. These officers are entrusted to make informed decisions about how best to serve those they represent while remaining faithful to the welfare of the entire Fellowship. As leaders they make decisions on how to better serve, but not on how to govern.

Beware of the group that becomes known as "so-and-so's" group. Under no circumstance should a group let a self-styled or elected leader make all its decisions. God does not rule through a king in a Twelve Step Fellowship. Neither does He direct through a divisive majority leaving a sizeable disgruntled minority.

God does not speak through those afflicted with the narrow vision of opinionated righteousness. We old-timers who feel too right to be wrong are usually too wrong to be right. Leaders who are trusted servants don't tell the group or Fellowship what to do. Sponsors do not tell those they sponsor what to do or not to do. We advise our leaders how to serve their Fellowship using the Twelve Steps and Twelve Traditions.

The group secretary, general service representative, steering committee, conference delegate, or office manager should not be the final authority on anything. They are but trusted servants elected or appointed to carry out the authority of a loving God as expressed through the unity of the group. That means there should nearly always be complete agreement among members on every group vote.

To insure the unanimity of any vote, members on investigating committees should be asked to thoroughly study the issues at hand by using all sources of information. The investigating committees consult the Fellowship's published literature and find out if the other groups have experienced similar problems in the past. The committees meet again, prepared to argue both sides, and then recommend a course of action.

There is no logical need for individual groups to suffer from mistakes already overcome by other groups. Memberships fully armed with facts rather than emotions fueled by ignorance usually arrive at near unanimity.

If nearly complete agreement cannot be achieved, it might be prudent for someone to make a motion to table the matter for further study.

As stated in Step Eleven, we must pray for knowledge of God's will for us and the power to carry that out. Only then will we be as Tradition Two suggests, a channel for God to "express Himself in our group conscience."

If in addition to placing your individual will and life in God's care you are willing to permit Him to be the ultimate authority of your entire Fellowship, you are already following Tradition Two. If you have joined the rest of us in this state of communal grace, you are ready to turn the page and have a look at Tradition Three.

TRADITION THREE

The only requirement for membership is a desire to stop our self-destructive behavior.

Does this mean an individual must stop his or her compulsive habit before joining the Fellowship? No, it does not. Whether an individual has succeeded in stopping has no bearing on his or her qualification for membership. To join a Twelve Step program a person need only want to stop.

For one person this desire may be to stop drinking. For another the desire may be to stop overeating. Many want to stop taking drugs or managing the lives of others. Maybe the desire is to stop gambling or spending too much money. Others still, want to stop trying to control their own emotions. The desire can be a wish to stop surrendering to whatever practice is preventing personal happiness.

Does a newcomer have to prove his or her desire to stop before joining a Fellowship? The answer is no. The newcomer need only express the desire to stop. Membership is not decided by a group or a Fellowship; only God has the ultimate ability to help people change their lives.

Originally, the only requirement for joining the Fellowship was *an honest desire* to stop self-destructive behavior. The only person who can confirm that desire is the person who has it. Neither jury nor membership committee is needed. Those who declare themselves in, are in.

Unfortunately a lot of us come into a Fellowship with certain defects of character. Perhaps we are too self-righteous. Our poor opinion of ourselves requires us to put down other people. Perhaps our overblown egos require that new members should possess our self-styled virtues. Could it be that we are afflicted with an impatience that will not tolerate less than instant perfection from those who ask us for help?

The General Service Conference of A.A. amended Tradition Three to eliminate the word *honest*. The only requirement for membership in A.A. today is a simple "desire to stop drinking."

Is it necessary for members of A.A. to identify themselves as alcoholics or for members of Narcotics Anonymous to say they are addicted to drugs? The answer is no. If you don't believe you are an alcoholic but would like to stop drinking, A.A. welcomes you. For those who aren't sure their sex and love problems are an illness but would like help in forming happier relationships, the arms of S.A.L.A. are open.

In many Fellowships, members identify themselves and their disease before speaking to the group. The E.A. member says, "I'm Susan and I'm powerless over my emotions." Labeling oneself aloud with the name of the disease is not a Tradition; it is a custom. Other people modify this custom by saying, "I'm Mary. I have a desire to stop using cocaine," or "I'm Peter and I want to cut down on my eating."

Those of us who need to conform to feel secure should resist the urge to force others to admit having diseases they are not certain they have. We should encourage honesty from the start rather than conformity. Many of us became members before we were able to do the First Step, admitting "we were powerless" over the substance or activity we wished to stop. By requiring newcomers to admit to their disease everytime they speak, we may be presupposing that they have accepted the First Step. Admitting powerlessness without believing it is lying. None of us wishes to encourage even a feeling of dishonesty in our "program of honesty."

The strangest bigotry to evolve since Alcoholics Anonymous was the only Twelve Step Fellowship, is a tendency by members of one recovery program to discriminate against dually-addicted members of other Twelve Step programs. Occasionally A.A. members have tried to deny membership to those with drug problems who want to stop drinking. Similarly, some Al-Anons have wanted to exclude A.A. members from attending Al-Anon meetings.

"We mustn't dilute our program by admitting those with problems different from our own," is the argument used against the dually-addicted. However, those who have a desire to stop self-destructive behavior have the right to membership in any Fellowship which addresses that specific problem. Whatever additional behavior another member desires to stop is none of our business.

There once were nonalcoholic spouses of A.A. members who, before Al-Anon was formed, wanted a Twelve Step program so badly they gave up social drinking to qualify as members in Alcoholics Anonymous. Their need to apply the Steps to their own part in the family illness gave them a desire to stop even nonalcoholic drinking. They had to attend A.A. meetings to learn how to apply the Twelve Steps to their own illness.

They were not spies or enemy invaders. They wanted so desperately to adapt A.A.'s recovery tools to their own illnesses, they did whatever was necessary to attend meetings. The desire to stop even harmless drinking made them welcome in A.A.

Many groups now exist whose names suggest that only certain people are eligible for membership. These groups challenge Tradition Three. Within one Fellowship someone started an Attorneys' Group. Someone else formed an Under-35 Group. These inspired other exclusive-sounding names such as the Young People's Group, Senior Citizens' Group, Business and Professional Group, Mexican-American Group, Men's Stag Group, and, of course, a Women's Stag Group.

Many such groups are in existence today in every anonymous Fellowship. Do they abide by Tradition Three that "the only requirement for membership is a desire to stop"?

Members of any sex, age, race, profession, or nationality are welcome. Tradition Three couldn't be clearer on this point.

Are you willing to accept for membership in your group a visitor from any of these other programs who has a desire to stop whatever you had to stop, no matter what that person's reason is for doing so? Are you ready to welcome as a new member, no questions asked, anyone who simply states the desire to stop?

If your hand is extended to welcome all such troubled strangers into your innermost circles of recovery, you are ready to turn the page and progress to the Fourth Tradition.

TRADITION FOUR

Each group should be autonomous except in matters affecting other groups or our Fellowship as a whole.

In Tradition Four autonomy means each group may conduct itself the way its members wish as long as it does not harm other groups or the Fellowship. Meeting formats may change from group to group, but the Twelve Steps remain the same. As long as a group voluntarily adheres to the Twelve Steps and Traditions, it may also raise funds in any way it chooses to pay bills and contribute toward expenses of the unified Fellowship.

Recognizing the autonomy part is only half the task involved in understanding and practicing Tradition Four. The second part of Tradition Four reiterates the message given in Tradition One, that our Fellowship functions as a whole.

I have attended Twelve Step meetings in 35 states of the U.S.A., eight Canadian provinces, and foreign cities such as Vienna and Hong Kong. I have been to meetings held for hundreds of members in Los Angeles, London, and Montreal. I have participated in discussion meetings in Tahiti and Mexico, with members numbering from two up to 100. Every meeting has been distinct.

My first meeting of a Twelve Step Fellowship was at Burbank, California in 1957. The meeting started with the Serenity Prayer followed by someone reading "How It Works" from the Big Book.* Next, a speaker gave a personal testimony. My second meeting was only 80 miles away in San Bernardino. It shook me up. They read a chapter from the Big Book and then sat around talking. Because they didn't run their meeting the same way my Burbank group did, I felt the San Bernardino people were "doing it all wrong." Fortunately, I didn't have the nerve to tell them how a group should conduct its meetings.

As Tradition Four points out, there is no set way a group is supposed to run its meetings. Any secretary of a new group will receive a variety of suggested formats from its national or world service office, but they are only suggestions. A group can set up a new format that nobody has tried as long as it doesn't threaten the welfare of any other group or the Fellowship as a whole. That is why, in one Fellowship, I can now find a candlelight meeting in Rapid City, South Dakota; a fireside meeting in Monterey, California; and a podium meeting in Beverly Hills.

Groups retain their autonomy, for example, in their prayer policies.

Most groups close meetings by joining hands and saying the Lord's Prayer. Some groups in British Columbia and elsewhere have decided by group conscience not to hold hands for fear it might intimidate newcomers into participating in a religious ceremony. Groups I have attended in England and Mexico didn't say the Lord's Prayer at all. Some groups conclude with the Serenity Prayer and other groups open with it. Many groups around the world simply ask a member to close the meeting by saying a prayer of his or her choice.

Members can choose to sit in rows, in circles on the floor, at tables, or hang from the chandeliers. It's up to the group.

---

*The Big Book is *Alcoholics Anonymous,* published by A.A. World Services, New York, N.Y. Available through Hazelden Educational Materials.

Each group may put on dances or banquets as it chooses. Members may celebrate birthdays and give out anniversary pins. Groups may read literature compatible with the Twelve Steps that is not "conference approved" as long as it is made clear to the members that it is not endorsed by the Fellowship. There is no such thing as conference disapproval.

The easiest way to violate a tradition is to not follow it. For example, when groups make decisions that threaten or neglect the welfare of the Fellowship as a whole, they are misusing the freedom set out for them in Tradition Four. Many times during the 29 years I have attended anonymous meetings, I have watched members debate whether to buy refreshments for the group or send funds to help support a central office.

Charismatic leaders and well-meaning members can manipulate a group, intergroup, general service committee, or district committee into enforcing a tradition that doesn't even exist.

An intergroup to which I was a delegate was once persuaded by an overzealous steering committee to forbid our central office from selling subscriptions to the Fellowship's monthly magazine. The intergroup acted because the magazine was not "conference approved." All Fellowship magazines are authorized for publication without "conference approval." Unfortunately, the groups did not practice enough autonomy to continue selling subscriptions to the magazine. Subscriptions in our district dropped off to nothing, which hardly contributed to "the welfare of our Fellowship as a whole."

A group which advises its members to attend certain meetings and to stay away from others can hardly qualify as being interested in the welfare of "other groups or our fellowship as a whole."

We must not only insist upon Tradition Four's autonomy for our group but also to grant it with love to other groups. The way to be free is to allow freedom. The way to guarantee autonomy is for each of us to mind our own group's business in accordance with the Twelve Traditions and do what we can to promote the Fellowship's well-being. If you can do that, it is time to turn the page and study Tradition Five.

TRADITION FIVE

Each group has but one primary purpose — to carry its message to the individual who still suffers.

Those of us most likely to forget the primary purpose of our groups are old-timers. Those of us who are recovering may find it easy to think the main reason for the group is to keep us well. "It's a selfish program," we are likely to say.

But is your Fellowship really selfish? I first realized that my program was not selfish while helping a sick ex-con in the smelly latrine of an east Oakland flophouse. I was on an after-midnight Twelve Step call. When I looked at the miserable place I was in and the foul-smelling stranger I was trying to help, it occurred to me that this was not a selfish thing I was doing.

Those of us who go to great lengths to help the still-suffering must have something other than selfishness going for us. We may be selfish as newcomers, but we do not remain that way. When we do the Seventh Step and "humbly asked Him to remove our shortcomings," let us hope that God will at least remove our selfishness.

We must remember to open up to visitors from out-of-town who have sought out our meetings. Those far from home who go to the trouble of finding a meeting in an unfamiliar location probably have more need to share experience and rebuild strength than do members snug and secure in the womb of their home group. Furthermore, the out-of-towner may have newer wisdom to contribute than we old-timers whose stories have been heard many times before.

Who would argue that common courtesy to sick newcomers or lonely visitors is not a good way for a group to fulfill its primary purpose, "to carry its message to the individual who still suffers"?

In trying to carry out Tradition Five, members sometimes misinterpret our primary purpose. A group may decide the best way to carry out the message is to become the biggest group in the area or the world. It may even have "talent scouts" attend beginners' meetings to recruit and swell its own membership. Preoccupation with being the biggest can become more important than merely spreading the message.

A group can also get carried away with controlling the behavior of newcomers as well as its regular members. Some groups require male newcomers to get haircuts and shave off their beards. I asked an old-timer from such a group why it treated new men that way. The old-timer looked squarely at my own beard of a dozen years and snapped, "So they can regain their self-respect!" I suggested he rename his program Beards Anonymous.

A well-intentioned group may order newcomers to refrain from sex for the first year. It may even try to keep a newcomer from going on dates during the first year. A group that concentrates on controlling the newcomer's behavior for an entire year is putting its own behavior modification program ahead of the Fellowship's Twelve Step program. For the group that teaches us to discipline ourselves rather than to "turn our will and our lives over to the care of God as we [understand] Him," the Steps are only a formality.

Placing rules in the way of the message would hardly be complying with Tradition Five. Putting requirements on members' personal appearance and social behavior is also out of tune with the Third Tradition that "the only requirement for membership is a desire to stop. . . ."

If a group chooses to use codes of personal behavior or appearance, it might be a good idea to announce at the start of each meeting that these recommendations are not those of the Fellowship as a whole, but are believed by "this particular group" to contribute to recovery. I have known sponsors who have dropped those they sponsor for not complying with the group's special suggestions.

Groups organized so that Fellowship members can get together to play bridge, bowl, attend the theater, go on camping trips, or ride motorcycles may be placing special interests ahead of spreading the message.

If your main interest in attending your group meeting is to learn how to recover and help others to recover, the group is safe in your hands. Others who feel as you do will help make sure the group's primary purpose continues to be "to carry its message to the individual who still suffers." If that's how you feel, you are in harmony with Tradition Five. Turn the page and take a look at one of the most interesting Traditions of all.

TRADITION SIX

A group ought never endorse, finance, or lend the Fellowship's name to any related facility or outside enterprise, lest problems of money, property, and prestige divert us from our primary purpose.

The word "endorse" used in Tradition Six means "to give sanction or support."

By this definition a hospital, recovery home, or club for recovering members should neither be permitted to use the Fellowship's name nor advertise that its treatment is based on the Fellowship's recovery program. Nor should a group or Fellowship give or lend money and become involved with the success or failure of such related facilities and outside enterprises.

Does this mean a Fellowship member should not donate money or volunteer time to spread the message to those in such facilities who still suffer? Of course not. What is suggested is that donations of time and money be made only on an individual basis. A group member should make it clear that such gifts are strictly personal and not from the Fellowship. Cooperation with the professional community is encouraged by all anonymous Fellowships, but cooperation does not constitute endorsement.

Does Tradition Six suggest that groups should not meet in hospitals, jails, recovery homes, or churches for fear of endorsing such institutions? Not at all. Tradition Four guarantees each group the autonomy to meet anywhere it chooses.

When I first moved to the Monterey Peninsula in California a group meeting in All Saints Church was listed in a Fellowship's directory as the "All Saints Group." Another group that met in a church called itself the "San Carlos Group." "The St. Dunstan's Group" met in another house of worship. A group that met in a recovery home called Beacon House called itself the "Beacon Rebound Group." Each name suggested affiliation with the institution it was renting space from. Informed group conscience of Tradition Six eventually resulted in each group renaming itself. The "All Saints Group" became the "Carmel Discussion Group," and so forth. The institution where meetings were held became part of the group's address, rather than its name.

One good reason for not endorsing related facilities is to ensure the attraction of all who have "a desire to stop" their destructive behavior. Catholics might be turned off by a group named after a Protestant church. Jews, Buddhists, or Moslems might reject a group whose name implies it is a Christian program. Nor will a group identifying itself with the Democratic party appeal to Republicans. In other words, a group or Fellowship ought to stand on its own two feet and represent only itself.

For years Alcoholics Anonymous committees worked to persuade the courts to recommend A.A. to alcoholic offenders rather than treat such diseased persons as criminals. This was finally worked out between local committees and enlightened judges.

Now, alcoholics brought to trial are often sentenced to attend A.A. meetings. The only way courts can reasonably enforce this is to require sentenced alcoholics to have proof-of-attendance slips signed at meetings. This simple system has resulted in vast numbers of additional alcoholics being exposed to the A.A. message. Not all have recovered, but thousands have.

Zealous "guardians of the Traditions" often find something

wrong with this system that works so well. They worry that signing "court slips" constitutes endorsement of the judicial system, which many of us have bad memories about. Some groups, without consulting their Fellowship literature or asking their general service office for information, refuse to sign slips for those sentenced to attend meetings. Fear of violating Tradition Six makes it impossible for sick people to comply with the law. Failure to return signed slips to a probation officer can result in imprisonment instead of spiritual recovery. Getting someone tossed into jail rather than welcoming him or her into A.A. hardly fulfills the Twelfth Step, "to carry this message to [other] alcoholics."

Overeaters Anonymous, Emotions Anonymous, Credit Card Anonymous, Cocaine Anonymous, Alcoholics Anonymous, and other thriving anonymous Fellowships have a lot in common, but they do not endorse each other. Smokers Anonymous, Gamblers Anonymous, and Al-Anon share the Twelve Steps and Twelve Traditions, but remain independent of one another. The Twelve Steps enable us to turn our lives over to God's care. The Twelve Traditions allow us to turn our group will over to Him and let Him run our autonomous Fellowships.

No one group owns an exclusive pipeline to God. The Twelve Steps and Twelve Traditions are protected by copyright but A.A. groups welcome other Fellowships to follow them. A.A.'s total group conscience found long ago that copyright laws do not make the Steps and Traditions its private property. Recovery programs that adhere to Tradition Six cooperate with one another, but do not endorse each other.

Tradition Six is specifically concerned with group behavior and the Fellowship's name. It does not apply to independently-acting individuals. A member acting on personal initiative may endorse, finance, or lend his or her own name to any facility or enterprise he or she chooses. An early technique of the National Council on Alcoholism was to provide a way for a movie star to publicly encourage alcoholics to seek help, without revealing the celebrity's A.A.

affiliation. Since the Fellowship was not mentioned in the media, there was no way to construe this as being out-of-sorts with Tradition Six.

A Twelve Step Fellowship collects and spends lots of money. It needs no financial problems other than its own. That is why social clubs for Fellowship members are set up as outside enterprises.

Fellowships do not operate hospitals or treatment centers. Institutions that teach paying patients a Fellowship's method of recovery support their own businesses without financial assistance from the Fellowship. Groups often meet in such places to attract patients into joining. As long as a Fellowship does not lend its name to the institution there is nothing wrong with carrying its message to those who still suffer. Nor does Tradition Six prevent a private recovery facility from urging its patients to join the Fellowship. Most do. It is only logical for local groups to keep the institution supplied with literature and meeting schedules to attract still-suffering victims.

A group may deliver its message anywhere as long as it does not endorse, finance, or lend its Fellowship's name to any related or unrelated facility. If you agree your group can cooperate yet not endorse religious organizations, treatment facilities, courts of justice, corporations, social clubs, and government projects, you are ready to turn the page and have a look at the Seventh Tradition which provides the hard cash necessary for your recovery.

TRADITION SEVEN

Every group ought to be fully self-supporting, declining outside contributions.

I know a group secretary who makes the following announcement at every meeting: "There are no dues or fees required for membership. We are passing the basket for you to put them in." The spiritual meets the material when the basket is passed. It costs money to have a meeting. A group must pay its rent, buy coffee, and purchase literature for newcomers. Groups must share the costs of an intergroup's central office. A central office secretary must be given a fair salary. Meeting schedules have to be printed. Postage has to be paid. Enough? Not quite.

Travel compensation should be given to group representatives and delegates who attend area meetings and national or world service conferences. Annual conference reports have to be reproduced and distributed. "My group should pay for all that?" a skeptic will ask. "Who else?" someone answers. And that's not all.

An overall service headquarters requires money to operate. It needs money to pay good staff workers. Literature must be published and distributed. The office must answer queries from individuals, hospitals, schools, prisons, doctors, and the clergy. Radio and TV announcements must be produced. All this requires cash. "Not from my group," a narrow-viewed member may object. "Each group should support itself, not the entire Fellowship."

But the entire Fellowship supports the group. Area, national, and world service levels are not independent entities. They are to the group what the heart is to the hand. There would not be groups without a Fellowship. Without the Fellowship there would be no recovery. A group which does not contribute money and ideas to all its Fellowship's levels of service is not truly self-supporting.

We can all dream up reasons for not dropping money into the basket. Being "broke" is the most common reason. Most of us managed to finance the illness that got us here in the first place. We raised enough money to pay for our disease. We did so with determination. Nothing could keep us from spending money on our addiction or compulsion. Reassigning a portion of the cash that kept us miserable is possible.

A treasurer I know who serves a Sunday morning A.A. meeting passes the basket while commenting that "the cost of a Bloody Mary at the local bar is now three dollars." She gets enough money in the collection to pay for the group's rent and refreshments and has enough to send to the central office, general service area, and general service office in New York. Her group is fully self-supporting, not because it pays for its own rent and coffee, but because it contributes its fair share to the entire Fellowship. It supports itself *and* its support system. That is what is meant by being *fully* self-supporting.

A group which accepts support from the Fellowship without contributing to the costs makes the Fellowship itself an outside contributor. We either pay for help or accept it from someone else. Groups which follow Tradition Seven pay their own way. They don't let other groups foot their Fellowship's bills for them. If they are too poor to contribute to the Fellowship's support system, they at least try to. They contribute what they can after making ends meet.

Groups or intergroups that don't raise enough money during regular meetings to pay their own way can raise it by holding fund-raisers. They can organize picnics, unity days, Step workshops, holiday marathon meetings, Tradition seminars, dances, banquets, weekend rallies, roundups, conventions, campouts, retreats, raffles, and other special events that will raise donations from Fellowship members. A little town in the Sierras named Susanville has only nine groups in one Fellowship. However, they manage to pay for a central office and secretary by putting on four fund-raisers each year. They earn enough money to contribute to their service area and world headquarters.

No Tradition discourages a group or intergroup from selling tickets to members for a fund-raising social event. However, Tradition Seven suggests such tickets not be sold to anyone outside the Fellowship.

For years groups have raised money from members by raffling off books. Rummage sales limited to Fellowship members have been held. Members have sold T-shirts, bumper-stickers, and posters to each other. There appears to be nothing unspiritual about using capitalist techniques to increase donations from Fellowship members. For a group to "go broke" rather than sell tickets within its Fellowship would be violating Tradition Seven.

"Outside contributions" means gifts of cash or materials from nonmembers of a Fellowship. The danger of exposing a group to pressure that might accompany contributions from government, institutions, or persons who don't belong to the Fellowship can be avoided by politely saying "no" to such offers of assistance.

Money left to a group or Fellowship in wills can be courteously rejected. Most Fellowships find it wise to limit the amount of money they will accept from any one of its own members, including bequests after death. This avoids any pressure that might accompany free cash.

A popular member of a Twelve Step program in my area died. His family requested that in lieu of flowers, donations be made in his name to his Fellowship. Checks mailed by mourners were politely returned with an explanation that the Fellowship does not accept outside contributions.

A military base by federal law cannot charge rent for a meeting space. A group I attend in an Army chapel pays its way by contributing to the coffee fund of the military personnel who work there. In Mexico, the organization who lent us space refused our rent money. We soon tired of insisting on paying rent to an organization that wouldn't accept it. We solved the problem by hiring someone to come in once a week to keep the place clean. Our hosts were delighted with our way of being self-supporting.

Oftentimes, several groups pool resources in order to rent a hall to share for their meetings. An old-timer I know challenges this practice as being against two Traditions. He maintains that pooling collections to pay for a meeting hall and common coffee supply violates Tradition Seven by keeping participating groups from being truly "self-supporting." In addition, he claims that this practice involves the groups in "matters of money and property," as discouraged by Tradition Six. However, groups jointly paying rent seem no more involved with money and property than those doing so individually. Pooling collections to make groups more securely self-supporting seems to satisfy the objective of Tradition Seven rather than abridge it.

Applying complete Traditions in solving problems is wiser than invoking parts of Traditions out of context. We ought to be careful not to apply one Tradition, and by so doing, preventing adherence to another. We must always try to keep the "primary purpose" stated in Tradition Five as our point of reference.

Once you understand why your group should try to be self-supporting, contribute to its Fellowship as a whole, and refuse outside donations, you are ready to turn the page and learn how Tradition Eight distinguishes between paid and unpaid service.

TRADITION EIGHT

Our Fellowship should remain forever nonprofessional, but our service centers may employ special workers.

"Nonprofessional" is an adjective defined in my dictionary as not "pertaining to an occupation pursued for gain." A professional fellowship would be one whose purpose is to make money.

A Twelve Step recovery Fellowship is not a profit-making enterprise. An anonymous program is not owned by individuals or stockholders. It charges no dues or fees for membership. It employs no psychologists, physicians, or practitioners to scientifically or religiously treat the disease its members recover from.

Members contribute what they can to support a Fellowship. There is a charge for books and pamphlets that carry the Fellowship's message of recovery, but money donated by members pays writers, typists, clerks, editors, bookbinders, shippers, and others needed to create and distribute effective literature that spreads the message. All these people are professional writers, professional typists, professional editors, and so on. They are professional in special skills for which they are gainfully employed by the Fellowship. The Fellowship itself is not their profession.

The first professional writer employed by a Twelve Step Fellowship was A.A.'s cofounder, Bill W. In his lifetime he received no compensation for founding or directing A.A. Bill probably did more Twelve Step work without pay than any other person in his day. He freely gave of his personal time and energy to spread the message. He was not a professional A.A. manager or speaker.

Bill received royalties for writing the books: *Alcoholics Anonymous, Twelve Steps and Twelve Traditions, A.A. Comes of Age,* and *As Bill Sees It.* This compensation made him a professional writer, not a professional Twelve Stepper. Royalty payments from sales of these books continue to go to Bill's heirs long after his death. Such payments are legitimate assets in a professional writer's estate. They are profits from the book, not from the Fellowship.

A Fellowship should no more expect a professional writer to write its books and pamphlets for free than it would expect a plumber to install a restroom at no charge, or a car dealer to donate a new automobile to the program.

Central office secretaries who manage an intergroup's local services are also "special workers." They should be fairly compensated for administrative skills and time required to serve both the public and local groups. They are paid workers, not paid officers.

Group secretaries, treasurers, intergroup delegates, district committee members, area officers, delegates to general service conferences, and trustees should never be paid. They usually are reimbursed for expenses incurred, but their services are donated freely out of gratitude to the Fellowships that saved their lives. Through them the group conscience of your Fellowship flows from you to the world headquarters and back again.

Some Fellowships are growing so fast large staffs of special workers are required to help them function in accordance with the Traditions. Trained workers organize books, type, operate computers, and handle the mail. Special workers that have professional skills are hired to coordinate programs in hospitals and institutions, disburse information to the public, cooperate with the professional community, produce and distribute literature, and keep a balanced budget. They are full-time salaried employees directed by professional general managers who in turn are guided by trustees, delegates, district committee members, and general service representatives. The one and only boss is God "as we [understand] Him."

Neither officers who "are but trusted servants" nor paid staff members who are "special workers" are in charge of the Twelve Steps.

Many paid workers are members of the Fellowships for which they work. After business hours, they can choose whether or not to donate their time and energy to do Twelve Step work with those who still suffer as they once did.

Does it violate Tradition Eight for a Fellowship member to take a job in a private recovery center? Hardly. Does an author who writes commercially published books about the program become a professional Fellowship member? Most certainly not. Does Tradition Eight discourage members from teaching about the disease and recovery? Not at all.

What purpose would it serve to prevent those who have recovered from being employed by related but nonendorsed facilities outside the Fellowship? Members of anonymous Fellowships probably know more about their diseases than many nonafflicted doctors, therapists, teachers, and clergy. Special knowledge acquired through their often bitter experiences enables recovered persons to become highly qualified professionals outside the Fellowship.

May members who are professionals outside the Fellowship "carry the message" of the Twelve Steps to paying clients or patients? Yes, they can. Some of the best alcoholism specialists in the world are physicians who belong to A.A. Outstanding weight-reduction counselors belong to Overeaters Anonymous. The founder of Emotions Anonymous was a psychology professor who has since authored best-selling books about how to handle emotional problems.

One of the cofounders of the granddaddy of all Twelve Step programs, Alcoholics Anonymous, was a doctor who professionally treated alcoholics for the rest of his life. The other cofounder authored the most personally profitable book on alcoholism ever written. It might be best if those of us who do not make professional contributions refrain from improperly invoking Tradition Eight's key word, "nonprofessional," to challenge those who do make professional contributions.

Those who ask your Fellowship for help should never be charged for it. A Twelve Step program may set prices for its literature but not for its services. Employees should be hired to manage the services, not the Fellowship.

If you agree that your Fellowship should operate along nonprofessional lines, you are ready to turn the page and learn how Tradition Nine enables the Fellowship to function and grow without being organized.

TRADITION NINE

Our Fellowship, as such, ought never be organized; but we may create service boards or committees directly responsible to those they serve.

Fellowships all over the world collect millions of dollars to pay for rent, refreshments, committee expenses, and special workers. Thousands of phones ring around the clock as suffering multitudes seek help. All the calls are answered. Books and pamphlets explaining recovery from dozens of addictions, diseases, compulsions, phobias, and obsessions are published, translated, and distributed around the globe.

Our Fellowship, as such, ought never be organized?

Impossible!

Or is it?

What qualities are found in most organizations?

People are in charge. Employees work under supervisors who are directed by a primary boss, who in turn is advised by a board of directors. Lieutenants and captains answer to majors and colonels who are obedient to field generals commanded by staff officers who are directed by the Joint Chiefs of Staff under orders given by the Commander in Chief. Or maybe a head surgeon issues orders to staff doctors who are in charge of interns who direct nurses that tell orderlies and receptionists what to do. Power structures are present in every major organization.

Rulers rule. Employees obey stringent rules laid on them by supervisors. Bosses obey privileged rules enforced by super-bosses.

People thrive on power. The ideal personal goal for many people is to advance to positions of power. Interns want to become doctors; colonels want to become generals. Employees want to become vice presidents so they can advance to the board of directors and take charge of the whole company.

Power invites politics. An employee's spouse has to shine up to a boss's mate. Department heads gossip to keep each other from being promoted. A relative moves up the corporate ladder faster than other qualified personnel. Someone who votes against the union is given a title and a raise. Everyone from building custodian on up to corporation vice president is scratching someone's back hoping for the same in return.

Profit is the bottom line. The formula for success used by most organizations involves receiving the most profit for the least amount of effort. Promotions are based on the size of profits rather than the quality of production. Those at the top live off the fat, while those struggling one rung at a time up the profit ladder salute it as "our way of life."

The dog-eat-dog approach seems to work for businesses, professions, governments, religions, schools, and charitable foundations. However, it won't do for a spiritual Twelve Step program of recovery.

New members have a hard time letting go of the old approach and accepting that "our Fellowship, as such, ought never be organized." It takes time for most of us to "turn our will and our lives over to the care of God." Eventually, however, we trust in a Power we can neither see nor hear to manage our entire Fellowship.

No member, secretary, general service representative, district committee member, delegate, trustee, or service office manager tells any other member, group, or committee what to do. Officers are organized to serve the Fellowship, not to govern.

Officers who "are but trusted servants" follow not rules, but the principles suggested in the Twelve Traditions. Their service binds the groups together in spiritual unity. Groups share experience, strength, and hope through these "trusted servants," without whom thousands upon thousands of autonomous groups would go their merry ways. Soon there would be little resemblance between them. There would be no common program of recovery.

Members within the Fellowship should not try to enforce the Traditions as if they were rules. The Twelve Traditions are suggestions for behavior just as the Twelve Steps are suggestions for recovery. Suggestions, not rules, saved the survivors of the *Titanic.* As the ship was sinking, the ship's crew suggested that passengers get into lifeboats. Tradition Nine suggests that we keep our Fellowship afloat by not organizing it.

Unlike organizations which exist for profits, our groups and Fellowships take care to make no profit other than their members' recoveries, grant no prestige other than mutual respect, with no motives greater than self-respect and care for other members.

Do you agree no member should be in charge, that there should be no rules or politics in your group or Fellowship, and that it should make no monetary profits? If so, you are ready to move on to Tradition Ten.

TRADITION TEN

Our Fellowship has no opinion on outside issues; hence the name of our Fellowship ought never be drawn into public controversy.

As we learned in Tradition Seven, we do not accept contributions from outside a Fellowship because we want to guard against being pressured by outside forces. In Tradition Ten we learn that we should also protect our Fellowship by not pressuring those on the outside.

Do you agree that your Twelve Step Fellowship is a winner? Your Fellowship was formed to address a deadly problem. It may have expanded into a worldwide Fellowship helping thousands to recover from incurable illnesses. Whether individual members win or lose depends entirely on whether they practice the principles of the program. The Fellowship itself never loses. It grows. No matter how many individuals fail to recover, more succeed. Word gets out. Those who stay and practice the Fellowship's Twelve Steps are winners. They win because the Fellowship is a winner.

Engaging in public controversy can make a loser out of a Fellowship. A champion who retires before risking one last contest remains an undefeated champion. A Fellowship has become champion by helping members defeat self-destructive behaviors. By taking sides on an outside issue, the Fellowship risks being on the losing team.

Occasionally some of us want to engage our Fellowship in a political cause because "we know more about it than anyone else." One may want to engage Alcoholics Anonymous in a campaign for a public treatment facility. Members of Narcotics Anonymous may want to help change drug laws. Gamblers Anonymous members may be in opposition to a state lottery referendum. No matter how good the cause or well-meaning our intent, standing up for one side or the other will upset the welfare of our Fellowship.

Let's say that a ballot issue we support wins. We automatically make ourselves political enemies of those who oppose it. Some opponents may be afflicted with our disease. Opposition to them on an issue could keep them from coming to us for help. Nobody wants to ask "the enemy" for assistance.

We should keep our individual Fellowships from becoming anyone's political enemy. The way to do so is to keep the Fellowships out of politics.

Does this mean a Fellowship member should not campaign for or against a political issue related to his disease or compulsion? Certainly not. This Tradition refers to Fellowship actions, not an individual's. It refers to the Fellowship name being used to support or discourage a public issue.

Tradition Ten is not intended to inhibit an individual member from engaging in political action motivated by personal conscience. Members of Twelve Step programs have run for political office at local, state, and national levels. In complying with Tradition Ten, they campaign without identifying themselves to the public as Fellowship members. Nor do they campaign during recovery group meetings.

What about controversy within a Fellowship? According to this Tradition our Fellowship should have no opinion on "outside issues." Yet even on inside issues "opinion" should not prevail. In accordance with the Second Tradition we already have an ultimate authority who expresses Himself through informed group conscience.

We are lucky. On our tough road to recovery, we can enjoy within ourselves the zest of combat and peaceful resolution. By protecting our own Fellowship from outside issues we can also avoid the agony of defeat.

If you believe your Fellowship's name should never be enlisted in support of outside causes or used as authority to settle public disputes, you are ready to turn the page and study the first of two Traditions regarding anonymity.

TRADITION ELEVEN

Our public relations policy is based on attraction rather than promotion; we need always maintain anonymity at the level of press, radio, and films.

When a professionally produced television announcement or radio spot broadcasts a Fellowship's name and phone number, new members sometimes react with bewilderment. "Isn't that against the Traditions?" they ask.

They can also be confused when members identify themselves at meetings by using their first and last names. "Hey!" the newcomer may respond. "I thought this was an anonymous program."

According to the dictionary, public relations are those "activities and techniques used by organizations and individuals to establish favorable attitudes and responses on their behalf on the part of the general public." Therefore, by definition, "activities and techniques" should be used by our Fellowship to favorably impress the public and attract new members who want to recover from self-destructive behavior.

I once moved into a community where a Fellowship's anonymity was so secure and its public relations so reserved it took me months to find its meeting place. And I was an experienced member. Any still-suffering person who didn't happen to know someone in the secret circle had no chance of finding it at all.

Within a year after that tiny group listed itself in the newspaper and yellow pages, it grew to include seven meetings a week.

"Attraction rather than promotion" doesn't mean "don't advertise." The question is, how do we advertise? Which techniques do we use? And which ones don't we do?

Twelve Step programs do not promise to treat or cure anything. They don't compete with any other programs or philosophies. They use no hard-sell techniques. Their advertising doesn't try to convince. They employ no such techniques of promotion.

Anonymous Fellowships offer help to those who suffer from specific problems. They advertise phone numbers and addresses for further information. They provide free literature to doctors, hospitals, jails, schools, and individuals. Fellowships and groups list themselves in newspapers and telephone books.

Tradition Eleven doesn't tell us to use only first names. The anonymity clause applies to the first part of the sentence, which is public relations. When making ourselves available to the public as Fellowship members, we don't use last names or show our faces. This is not only to protect the individual from being exposed as having a problem, it is also to keep the Fellowship from being publicly identified with the individual.

Because there may be as many interpretations of the Twelve Step recovery program as there are members, the anonymity clause is to keep members from being identified by the public as spokespersons for their Fellowship. Without this clause someone's personal view of his or her program may be mistaken as more valid than someone else's view. We wouldn't want that.

Another purpose of media anonymity is to insure against the public concluding that the Twelve Steps don't work if a famous member should relapse into self-destructive behavior.

One more aim of Tradition Eleven is to keep members who are authors from misleading the public into thinking their independently written and published books are endorsed by the Fellowships they belong to. Authors comply by not revealing in print which particular Fellowships they are members of.

Does Tradition Eleven imply that members should not be interviewed by the press or participate in broadcasts that discuss the Twelve Step program? Not at all. Tradition Eleven suggests that care should be taken in such instances not to reveal last names or faces. Holding meetings on the air is sometimes used as a technique to attract new members. It's easy to remain anonymous on radio by using first names only. On TV faces can be hidden in silhouette or deep shadow. I once took part in a show in which the video camera focused only on the laps of a Fellowship's members. An upsurge of newcomers can be attracted to a Fellowship when anonymous members participate in talk shows.

A less glamorous way to attract new members is to maintain free literature racks in doctors' offices, hospitals, recovery homes, jails, police stations, and health spas. Groups can post meeting notices on public bulletin boards at supermarkets, colleges, senior citizens' centers, and hospitals.

By sitting around waiting for someone to walk through the doorway, groups are not practicing Tradition Five: to spread the message to those who still suffer. Effective attraction is hard work.

"To recover you've got to stay willing," an old-timer from Laguna Beach likes to say. "In our program everyone is willing. Ten percent are willing to do all the work, and ninety percent are willing to let them." Not putting out the effort to attract newcomers is a break with the Tradition.

Dr. Bob said first and last names should be used within the group. He posed an intelligent question. How can members who need help find you if they don't know your name?

According to Dr. Bob, using only first names at the group level is as much against the spirit of the Fellowship as it would be to use full names in the press, radio, and film.

Dr. Bob's cofounder, Bill W., was about as anonymous at the public level as Jesus C. The need to remain publicly anonymous was realized years too late for Bill to escape fame as a founder of the first Twelve Step recovery program. But he tried. Once Tradition Eleven was firmly established, Bill reluctantly turned down an honorary doctorate from one of the world's great universities to avoid having his name proclaimed as founder of the most successful recovery program in history. When addressing a meeting of their Fellowship, Dr. Bob S. and Bill W. rarely refrained from identifying themselves by their first and last names.

I was recently told that a member named John had died.

"John who?" I asked.

"You know . . . John in San Francisco."

Finally, Fellowship officers should use their full names so that members can find them when they need service. I know some who believe that officers who list their first and last names, addresses, and phone numbers in membership directories are violating Tradition Eleven. The same people think their Fellowship violates a Tradition by collecting a registration fee at its World Convention. No such Tradition exists. I hope this book helps clear up such misunderstandings.

Do you believe your Fellowship should advertise information telling people where to get help if they need it? Do you agree that names and faces should not be used in public media to increase membership? Can you be comfortable when members reveal their last names during meetings or in your Fellowship's service literature?

If your answer to these questions is yes, you are ready to turn the page and move on to the last Tradition which is also concerned with anonymity.

TRADITION TWELVE

Anonymity is the spiritual foundation of all our Traditions, ever reminding us to place principles before personalities.

Are we being humble when we take all the credit for our own or someone else's recovery? Humility is acquired by working through the Twelve Steps and realizing that a Power greater than our own is responsible for our recovery. Anonymity reminds us to "place principles before personalities." Anonymity, humility, and spirituality go hand in hand.

In Tradition Eleven we learned why remaining anonymous at the public media level allows the Twelve Steps to speak for themselves. The Twelve Steps have become famous. Those who deliver the message of the Steps don't become famous as members of a Fellowship for doing so. Those who deliver the message of a particular Fellowship should remain anonymous so its newcomers will not confuse celebrity with the twelve principles that have helped millions recover from incurable illnesses.

When newcomers hear about a Twelve Step Fellowship they are often most attracted by the word, Anonymous. Anonymity assures us that no one will find out we have "sunk so low." Although our addiction or compulsion was once our source of comfort, it eventually became our source of misery, driving us to seek a Twelve Step recovery program. At first, our feelings of desperation seemed so shameful a defeat that we often feared most that family, friends, and business associates would find out about our problem.

Knowing that anonymity will be respected in Twelve Step groups helps newcomers commit themselves to recovery. They can feel sure that when they walk in that door no one "outside" will find them out. Newcomers and members alike feel safe knowing that whatever they say will be kept confidential by the other members. The warm embrace of assured anonymity is the first hint of the spiritual comfort and feeling of well-being that will gradually be provided by a Power greater than ourselves.

Competition and anonymity don't go well together. Groups could hardly be more spiritual than individuals seeking big-shot status. A competitive group sometimes becomes known by the name of its founder or guiding personality. A group known as "Joe's group" or "Francey's group" may not be adhering too well to Tradition Twelve's spirit of anonymity. One way for a group to protect its "spiritual foundation" of anonymity is to never compete with other groups.

The great psychologist, Carl Gustav Jung, thought that practicing alcoholics were unconsciously seeking God by drinking spirits. *Spiritus contra spiritum* or "Spirit against spirit" was the formula Jung prescribed as the only means by which an alcoholic could recover. Spirit against spirit can be more accurately translated as, "the spirit of God against the false spirit, alcohol." The same spirit will conquer other compulsions.

To the questions posed at the beginning of the chapter, Are we being humble when we take all the credit for our own or someone else's recovery? — the answer is no. We are humble when we admit that God is the reason for our recovery; remaining anonymous encourages us to submit to His Power and thank Him for doing what we could not have done alone.

As a personal reminder I keep a note pasted to my mirror where I can find it first thing in the morning. It reads:

> Dear Joe. . .
> I don't need your help
> today.
> Love,
> God

USING THE TRADITIONS

Could a corporation operate effectively using the Twelve Traditions? Maybe not. I don't know if anyone has ever applied them to a corporate setting. But for a recovery program based on the psychic transformation of its members, the Twelve Traditions work very well.

Individual Fellowships have adapted the Traditions to fit their specific needs. Al-Anon has changed Tradition Two from "there is but one ultimate authority," to "there is but one authority." Al-Anon members felt that by referring to the authority of an "ultimate" power they were still tempted to seek authority other than God's. The original version would not have been appropriate for those who are compulsive managers.

Minor changes or additions suiting the special needs of various Fellowships have been edited into Traditions. However, the Traditions address the same problems of all recovery groups in the same way. Arguments about slightly different wording are probably harmless as long as the spiritual purpose remains identical.

All walks of life cooperate in a very special way when they follow the Twelve Traditions. People of divergent religions and philosophies blend together in a common state of grace. All allow an undefined Higher Power to take control. All races harmonize in following the Twelve Traditions. The Traditions bridge all generation gaps from Alatots and Alateens to senior citizens groups. This magic code of behavior works without fail for all Fellowships that thoroughly follow its guidelines.

If our Fellowships are not held together by rules, what does hold them together? What makes Twelve Step recovery programs run so efficiently?

The answer is in how we come together. We share problems with others who have the same problems. We needn't speculate about how the other person feels. We know because we have been there, too.

We experience the same kind of recovery by following the identical Twelve Steps. We care about each other because we identify with one another's pain and happiness. We love each other.

The magic cement that binds our Fellowship together is love. By eliminating all barriers of human ambition, the Twelve Traditions of love allow our Fellowship to accept the gifts of God. The Twelve Traditions are to the group what the Twelve Steps are to the individual. Through the Twelve Steps God provides recovery. Our Twelve Traditions unite us as instruments of His love. A power-seeking person offers little to the group except the problems of his or her egotism. An overambitious group gives little to the individual except more of what should have been left outside in a power-troubled world.

THE TWELVE TRADITIONS*

1. Our common welfare should come first; personal recovery depends upon A.A. unity.

2. For our group purpose there is but one ultimate authority — a loving God as He may express Himself in our group conscience. Our leaders are but trusted servants; they do not govern.

**Twelve Steps* and *Twelve Traditions*, published by A.A. World Services, Inc., New York, N.Y. Available through Hazelden Educational Materials.

3. The only requirement for A.A. membership is a desire to stop drinking.

4. Each group should be autonomous except in matters affecting other groups or A.A. as a whole.

5. Each group has but one primary purpose — to carry its message to the alcoholic who still suffers.

6. An A.A. group ought never endorse, finance, or lend the A.A. name to any related facility or outside enterprise, lest problems of money, property, and prestige divert us from our primary purpose.

7. Every A.A. group ought to be fully self-supporting, declining outside contributions.

8. Alcoholics Anonymous should remain forever nonprofessional, but our service centers may employ special workers.

9. A.A., as such, ought never be organized; but we may create service boards or committees directly responsible to those they serve.

10. Alcoholics Anonymous has no opinion on outside issues; hence the A.A. name ought never be drawn into public controversy.

11. Our public relations policy is based on attraction rather than promotion; we need always maintain personal anonymity at the level of press, radio, and films.

12. Anonymity is the spiritual foundation of all our traditions, ever reminding us to place principles before personalities.